Sister Painter:

Misogynoir, Intersectionality, and Black British Women's Painting

Tilda Williams-Kelly

An imprint of Boom Publications Ltd

272 Bath Street
Glasgow SCOTLAND
G2 4JR

Boom Graduates and the logo are trademarks of Boom Publications Ltd.

Boom Publications Ltd is a more-than-profit company, dedicating over half our profits to university scholarships for underprivileged students worldwide. In order to offset our carbon footprint, we also pledge to plant a tree for each graduation book commissioned.

Sister Painter
was first published in Great Britain in 2022.

Copyright © Tilda Williams-Kelly. Tilda Williams-Kelly has asserted her right under the Copyright, Designs and Patents Act, 1988,
to be identified as Author of this work.
For legal purposes any Acknowledgements constitute
an extension of this copyright page.
Cover design by Boom Graduates Ltd and the Book Cover Zone USA.

All rights are reserved. No part of this publication may be reproduced or transmitted in any form or by any means, electronic or mechanical, including photocopying, recording, or any information storage or retrieval system, without prior permission in writing from the publishers.

Boom Publications Ltd do not have any control over, or responsibility for any third-party websites referred to or in this book. All internet addresses given in this book were correct at the time of going to press. The author and publisher regret any inconvenience if addresses have changed or sites have ceased to exist, but can accept no responsibility for any such changes.

Typeset by Helen at Boom Graduates.
Printed and bound in the UK.
To find out more about our authors and books visit www.boomgraduates.com
and sign up for our newsletters.

Sister Painter

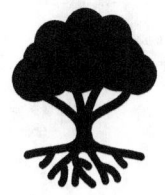

We plant a tree for every
Boom Graduate book commissioned, and
thereafter plant a tree for every 10 books sold!

THG

(more : trees)

MEMBER

Watch our forest grow at
https://moretrees.eco/forest/BoomPublicationsLtd/

Tilda Williams-Kelly

Sister Painter

Tilda Williams-Kelly

Contents

Author biography 9
Abstract 11
Foreword 15
Introduction 19
Chapter 1 19
Chapter 2 27
Chapter 3 35
Chapter 4 43
Conclusion 51
Appendix 1 57
Appendix 2 59
Appendix 3 61
Appendix 4 63
Appendix 5 65
Appendix 6 67

Appendix 7	69
Appendix 8	71
Appendix 9	73
Appendix 10	75
Bibliography	77
Artist's images	91
Acknowledgements	105
A note about Boom Graduates	107
BOOM!	111
Notes	113

Author biography

Tilda Williams-Kelly (she/her) b.1999 is a Scottish visual artist based between Alloa and Glasgow. Tilda's practice involves portrait and figurative oil painting, open to myriad avenues of expression, producing vibrant and impactful images that explore themes of colour, light, environment and humanity.

This humanity begins with the self; what began as a reckoning with the notion that only men can paint, has morphed into an inner search of her own Trinidadian and Irish lineage, and the role of Scottish colonialism as a Scottish artist with this lineage. Tilda's work is to convey the necessity in uplifting one another; she looks to community as sources of inspiration and strength. Pursuits are based in community arts activism, collaboration, and research within socio-political settings such as anti-racism, intersectional feminism, and climate justice.

Tilda blends classical oil techniques with contemporary style in both reference and countering with the oil 'masters' that first inspired her to pursue an oil portrait practice. Tilda takes this classical method, and manipulates it to speak to us in the present; merging their methods with spray painting, mark making, abstraction and imagination is Tilda's way of expressing blackness and joy. She skilfully engages storytelling and mythos to address histories of erasure and subjugation often visited on Black bodies. In opposition to this, she chooses to represent the Black figure in compositions that evoke a sense of liberation and inner strength.

Abstract

Studies show that white male chauvinism persist in the arts. This faces female Black, Indigenous, and People of Colour (BIPoC) artists with a dilemma of intersectional discrimination within education, galleries, museums, and the art market. Research into the *British Black Arts Movement* (1980s) reveals that BIPoC artists' contributions are ignored within art history and underrepresented in mainstream visual arts institutions. Research into recent feminist academia show that women are also lacking from senior positions within art institutions as well as undervalued within the market (late 20th century-present). This study aims to underline the necessity for a continuation of activism for Black women's creative discourse as first expressed by the women involved in the 1980s *British Black Arts Movement*.

The methodology research for this book has operated under reflective practice and reflexivity, a process enlisted with the aims of developmental change within education organisations (Gould 2004). Although reflective methods can be described as 'soft and unquantifiable' (Regan 2008, p.219), it is necessary to employ so-called 'contradictory' terms like 'creative' and 'analytical' as they are inevitable (Richardson and St Pierre 2005, p.962) because experiences are not saved as data (Winter 1988 p. 235). These methods allow for protected exploration on easily contradicted topics such as damaging social and cultural biases, inequalities, and silenced marginalised voices.

Research by notable animateurs such as Maud Sulter b.1960 and Lubaina Himid b.1954, feminist scholars and historians Helen Gørrill b.1969 and Griselda Pollock b.1949, art historians Kobena Mercer b.1960 and Eddie Chambers b.1960, and black feminist scholars such as bell hooks b.1952 and Audre Lorde b.1934, indicate a critical gap in our knowledge of BIPoC and women's contributions to art history, and the particular discrimination felt by Black women globally due to intersectional discrimination.

Tilda Williams-Kelly

Foreword

There are four important caveats in this book which must be addressed: Firstly, the identifier 'British' will be used throughout this essay, although almost all artists discussed are affiliated with England, it is doubtful they would refer to themselves as English due to repercussions of colonial rule and would likely prefer e.g., 'Ghanaian-British'. Secondly, as a Scottish art student my interests lie in a Scottish perspective of Black art. However, in order to address the histories of black art within a British context, a focus solely on Scotland would exclude almost all of the critical engagement necessary for this paper. Thirdly, the use of 'Black' capital B[1] must be explained. A term

---

[1] We use 'black' lowercase b to describe people of the African diaspora – that is African and Caribbean ancestry. 'Black' capital B is a little more complicated within a UK context.

popularised in the late 1970s and 1980s describes *all* visible ethnic minorities. This included, but was not limited to, people of African, South Asian, Arab, and Caribbean descent. This was a political identifier used across the UK and by visual artists themselves. Throughout this essay 'Black' will not be used as an umbrella identifier, except when referring to the exhibitions/collectives at the time of its relevance, and black lowercase will be used to describe people of African and Caribbean descent. The use of the terms Black and Indigenous People of Colour (BIPoC), and women of colour (WOC) describe people and women respectively who are visible ethnic minorities. Fourthly, we must acknowledge that these 1980s collectives largely ignored the specific experiences of South Asian artists in favour of a unified message of anti-racism. The South Asian experience[2] deserves critical analysis of its own; art historian

---

[2] In-depth insight and research particular to the experience of e.g., South Asian/Asian women, is equally important. However, in keeping with word count, and encompassing reflexivity methods, my focus is personal to my experiences, practice and activist pursuits that I am attempting to engage in.

Dr Alice Correia's *Researching Exhibitions of South Asian Woman Artists in Britain in the 1980s* (2019)[1] provides an in depth and more appropriate analysis than I am able to give here.

Tilda Williams-Kelly

Introduction

Chapter 1

Literature Review

Academics Eddie Chambers b.1960[20] (2014) and Stuart Hall b.1932 [21] (2005/6) have provided useful timelines to the history of Black British artists. For topical context a summary of British Black art must be made, however in keeping with this book's limited word count and focused relevance, these texts are summed up to a very small degree. Stuart Hall (2005/6) surmises Black British art as three 'moments' or 'waves'.[22] The first being the post-war 'colonials' who travelled to Britain following the fall of the British Empire and assurances of de-colonisation, eagerly joining the 'new, modern world'. The second 'wave' spans the late 1970s and 1980s and includes the children of the first, and later arrivals, who effectively solidified the notion of Black art, with collectives such as the *Blk Arts Group* (1979) and the wider *British Black Arts Movement* (1982). Two exhibitions compiling histories were *The Other Story* (1989) curated by Rasheed Araeen, and *Transforming the Crown: African, Asian and Caribbean Artists in Britain 1966-1996* curated by Mora Beachamp-Byrd. Collaboration was based on political alliance and challenging dominant Western Eurocentric values in art culture, and addressed the experiences of marginalised groups in Britain, with a strong focus on anti-racist activism. Of significant importance to the timing of this book, the third and final wave is emerging at this present time and is undoubtedly too soon to attempt to define.

The late 1970s and 1980s, increasingly recognised Black British artists, and the presence of the Black woman artist, that were, 'exhibiting together, as well as exploring issues of common concern and creativity together, without the sometimes stifling intervention of men.' (Lloyd 1986). [23] However, it is noted by Chambers the temporality of this [24] (p.128), supporting Hall's use of terminology like 'moments' and 'waves', we get the impression this was a spirited yet fleeting revolution that quickly settled, a sentiment soberingly echoed by Lubaina Himid; '...all of us destroyed it. We cannot revisit it except as a dead thing to worship or be nostalgic about' [25] (2005).

A Black homosexual identity also emerged, filmmaker Isaac Julien, and photographers Rotimi Fani-Kayode, Sunil Gupta and Ajamu formed a faction of the wider movement. Chambers notes that, 'certain people had argued that the 'struggle' had been located around 'masculinist' sensibilities, policed by heterosexual Black men' (Chambers 2014). [26] There are indications of this from other sources, Claudette Johnson asks 'Did the women write enough?' (2005) 27 and Keith Piper's texts surrounding Black masculinity, located his dehumanisation as athletic, musician, or thug, and also includes gender-polarisation, which he credits to the dismissal of women and homosexual Black experiences. (Mercer):[28]

> As a heterosexual Black man, I suspect that one of the reasons for this relative absence of an introspective voice is that, like heterosexual white men, we have been raised upon the assumption that somewhere along the line it is our job to 'manage' the planet.[29]

Art historian Kobena Mercer offers insight behind this 'oppressed becoming oppressor' matter; the 'black male antagonist' a prevalent character in popular media and music, (think Wesley Snipes' alter ego on the basketball court in *White Men Can't Jump*). This is an attempt at empowering black men under machismo to resist the attested emasculation of black men by white men (although black women are blamed for this emasculation).

Mercer concludes these 'black fantasies of empowerment ... nonetheless excluded our sisters and reinforced an inadequate either/or model of politics on account of its unthinking masculinism'. As this book is based around WOCs activities in the arts, regardless of sexuality, the treatment of gay black men, while equally valid, is not explored further.

This attitude from men of colour is indicative of the retrospectives supplied by Lubaina Himid, on the quietness surrounding the efforts of Claudette Johnson, 'who decided to take the women at the Black Art Conference into another space, in order for us to engage with the issues most important to us'. (p.43) This is necessary as Himid states the importance of Johnson within the *Blk Art Group*, she '[visually] said things about black women's bodies, experiences, aspirations that changed lives,' and was yet unrecognised by the male lens of the movement; 'Stuart Hall never mentioned her. Rasheed Araeen did not talk about her. Keith Piper did not speak her name' (Himid, 2005).[30]

Three exhibitions curated by Lubaina Himid, ushered in the supposed era of Black women's innovation. The first being *Five Black Women Artists* (1983) at the Africa Centre, in London, followed by *Black Woman Time Now* (1983-4) at the Battersea Arts Centre, and the third, *The Thin Black Line* (1985) at the Institute for Contemporary Arts in London. Himid pulled these off with very little funding; *Five Black Women Artists* was put together without a fee for the artists or curator. The Africa Centre itself did not gain financially from the show either. Similarly, *Black Woman Time Now* was curated without any money for the artists, selector, for transport or for the catalogue. The Arts Centre itself did however gain a wider audience and reputation.

The Thin Black Line was 'blessed' with a little money, for six months of organising Himid received just £250.[31] (See appendix 7 for full list of those involved).

Musings on the period are still going to this day, later stated fiercely by Himid, these women were, 'not a movement, or a group or a sisterhood or even close friends but instead a fluid set of women who were not prepared to be herded into a single way of expressing [them]selves.' (Himid 2012) [32] With this in mind, Himid collaborated with Maud Sulter on numerous pursuits from the beginnings of the *Blk Arts Group*, to Sulter's too-soon death.

Maud Sulter, Scottish-Ghanaian Glasgow-born fine artist, educator, curator and writer, whose photography project *Sphinx 1987* documented St. James Island,[33] which was used as a shipping post for African men, women and children who were subjected to slavery. Sulter has contributed a great deal to the histories of British colonialism, and furthermore, supported the voices of the women involved in her collection of essays, images and poems in *Passion: Discourses on Blackwomen's Creativity*, which provides enlightening insight to the thoughts of these animateur women. Her involvement with the movement and unique perspective as the only noted Scot within, makes her pivotal in intersectional feminist critique, UK race issues and Scottish perspective of both, and yet has been consistently left out of Scottish art education (Bernier, 2018).[34]

Tilda Williams-Kelly

Chapter 2

Misogynoir and Intersectionality

*Each of us is responsible for everything
and to every human being
(Simone de Beauvoir)*

Misogynoir, like misogyny, is rarely recognised as it is often subtle and acceptable. Misogynoir is a relatively new term, but it is not new. African American abolitionist and activist Sojourner Truth referenced misogynoir in her legendary speech at the 1851 women's rights convention in Arkon Ohio, where she asked, 'Ain't I a woman?'[35] (hooks 1981). For modern examples of misogynoir, as mentioned, is exemplified in the disproportionate abuse of MP Dianne Abbot by both British media and the public[36] (Palmer 2020), who in the run up to the 2017 UK election received 45.14% of *all* abusive tweets directed at politicians[37] (Dhrodia 2017), (See appendixes 8-11).

The importance of representation is explained by art critic John Berger in *Ways of Seeing*, as it is in imagery that the conditions of lives are determined[38] (2008), and a lack of true representation leads to harmful distortions. Misogynoir is often a reaction to such distortions perpetuated in ignorance, however, it originated through intentional actions. Initially, sexualised animalistic depictions were used to justify the raping of slave women[39] (bell hooks, 1981), the 'mammy' character emerged as early as 1852; unintelligent, subservient and undesirable, she was used to placate the white woman of the households' she usually worked in. [40] The 1920s tv-show *Amos 'n' Andy* was responsible for the premier of 'Sapphire', she berated and emasculated black men, launching the persistent trope of the 'angry black woman'[41] and propagating a contempt of black women by black men. The 1970s saw the *blaxploitation* era, where fantasies of hyper-sexual rebels exacted revenge, aiding in the notion of black women as both threatening and promiscuous.

In modern media 'the strong black women,' was created by black women to provide a positive depiction in contrast to earlier portrayals. This one-dimensional representation also causes serious harm. It dictates that black women must never appear 'weak,' or seek help[42] (Leath 2019) which according to the BBC makes them less likely to seek medical treatment. Black people in Britain have the lowest rate of mental health treatment[43] (*Mental Health Foundation* 2018) despite black women being more likely to suffer from depression and anxiety than white women (Cooper et al 2010).[44]

Black women are perceived as significantly more aggressive, unintelligent and tough by healthcare professionals, so complaints of pain are more likely to be ignored, and this has lethal consequences. In the UK, black women are *five times* more likely to die in childbirth than white women[45] (2018). I myself, the youngest of three, was born at home, in direct avoidance of hospital treatment, in response to humiliating and dehumanising treatment my mother was subjected to, by healthcare staff, during her previous pregnancies (Leicester General Hospital, 1994 and 1995).

Oppressive structures based on sex and race are maintained through the division and mistrust between those that do not benefit. With men centred in anti-racism movements and white middle-class women in feminism, often black women were left entirely out of the conversation, which began to change with the emergence of the concept of 'intersectionality'.

The aesthetic value of women's artworks has long been questioned, German artist Georg Baselitz claimed in *Der Spiegel*[46] magazine (2013), 'women don't paint very well. It's a fact,' evidenced by their failure to pass the 'market test.' Indeed, women make up 2% of the market, a proportion which has doubled in a decade[47] (Halperin and Burns, 2019). Women's work sells for significantly less than men's, with highest valued painting by a man being David Hockney's *Portrait of an Artist (Pool with Two Figures) 1972*, which sold for

$90.3 million (£67.85 million) in November 2018, comparatively Jenny Saville's *Propped 1992*, sold the previous month for £9.5 million, just 14% of the cost of Hockney's. Since 74% of fine art students are women (Gørrill 2020)[48], this points to a troubling disparity in the appreciation of creative practices between men and women.

These disparities lead to a mistrust in the system and in one's own abilities, self-fulfilling prophecies that can then be applied as evidence of a meritocratic industry. As art critic Brian Sewell argues, to charge women artist's abysmal marketable value to gender politics is, 'too simplistic', yet he also states, 'only men are capable of aesthetic greatness' (2008). This type of roundabout logic propagates the disillusionment in women's abilities, as Maud Sulter stated:

> The endeavours and successes of Black women's creativity are often criticised but seldom critiqued in a constructive upwards and outwards way. This leads to a fear of discourse and dialogue which undermines our aims and must be countered (Sulter, 1990).[49]

Quantitative data can be helpful to counter these claims, a strategy used and explored by academic Helen Gørrill, supported by feminist writer Maura Reilly and by the *Guerrilla Girls* (Gørrill 2020).[50] *The Black Artists and Modernism National Audit Collection* led by Dr Anjalie Dalal-Clayton, found that there are just 2,000 artworks by black artists in the UK's permanent collection, most not displayed (2020).[51] Quantitative data has contributed to a broad acknowledgement of sexism in the arts. Attempts at dismantling systematically bigoted structures elicit a response of weariness, and violent dismissal from those who occupy the norm (Hardi 2020). A helpful analysis of this was made by philosopher John Stuart Mill, who stated, 'Everything which is usual appears natural. The subjection of women to men being a universal custom, any departure from it quite naturally appears unnatural' (1869).[53] Like Sojourner Truth's assessment of misogynoir, there is nothing *new* about these societal conclusions and yet they remain largely unchallenged by those with hegemonic power.

The time for naivete and inculpability has long passed, as Himid alluded, the defensive and wilfully ignorant have proved unreliable, as emphasis on our differences has historically divided us as a human race, Lorde ponders, 'It is [these] distortions which separate us. And we must ask ourselves: Who profits from all this? (1984).[54] I would suggest, in answer to this question, we refer to *All the Presidents Men* and simply, *follow the money*.

Tilda Williams-Kelly

Chapter 3

Aesthetics and Communication

Your spur to creation is the desire to communicate

(Sulter 2008)[55]

The women involved in the 80s *Black Arts Movement* were committed to the establishment of WOC in contemporary arts, and they 'did not think about audiences in the same way or use materials the same way. [They] prioritised differently in relation to politics, money or faith and were brave enough to expose this' (Himid).[56] However, in researching selected painting practices, and statements, of prominent WOC artists, we can detect certain affinities that they share, implying the presence of a dialogue that tells us their aims as both artists and political activists.

In the work of Lynette Yiadom-Boakye b.1977, we see a commitment to the dignified in her earthly hued figurative painting of dark ambiguous figures. Other artists might opt to employ a diasporic style in portrayals of black figures, such as Jean-Michel Basquiat's skeletal men who bare teeth from stripped away flesh,[57] or Chris Ofili who pays homage to the stereotyping of black women with their exaggerated features stretched over warped curved bodies.[58] Combining writing and painting practice, Yiadom-Boakye has built a charmed world that welcomes black people as introspective, boisterous and contemplative.[59]

Confirming that '[she doesn't]…like to paint victims'[60] Yiadom-Boakye's figures gaze out of windows, men in sharp green suits chuckle together, a playful cat is settling on a man's orange turtleneck and ballerinas gracefully plié. Like Yiadom-Boakye, Claudette Johnson's figures centre the frame, which serves as solely a window for the viewer, they live beyond its constraints, often stretching limbs out of sight. Clothed, nude, sombre or joyful, they are proud and unapologetic.[61] Themes of sexual liberty, menstruation and vulnerability run throughout her work, as she explains, Johnson's commitment is to portraying the realities of the lives of black women.

> ...I'm not interested in portraiture or its tradition. I'm interested in giving space to Blackwomen presence. A presence which has been distorted, hidden and denied. I'm interested in our humanity, our feelings and our politics... (Johnson).[62]

Humanity is exemplified in *Big Woman's Talk* where Sonia Boyce (b.1962) presents her child self, resting on her mother's lap while the 'big women talk' in the domestic embrace of a Caribbean household. Bringing the lives of these Caribbean women to the public sphere, this painting is quite lovely in its success of conveying strong emotional ties to home life that would rarely be seen in British media. Use of pattern alludes to West Indian homes, and lilac colours throughout, most notably reflected in the eyes of the child-Boyce is indicative of a pleasant hazy memory.

Similar to Johnson's rejection of tradition, Sonia Boyce is 'very adamant, despite the fact that [her] drawings look like paintings, that [she is] not a painter,'[63] placing more importance on drawing; methods thought of as the base for 'mature' pieces in oil. Boyce considers 'working with these undervalued forms [as] an open challenge to the dominance of traditional art'[64] (Bernier 2018), and 'resists the idea of painting as all important and of drawing as subsidiary' (Carey-Thomas, Goodwin, 2012). Confident in critiquing the established framework set in place by eras of a monopolising 'intellectuality', as a black woman, she has been historically excluded from the fine arts, confirming the rationality in rooting black art in the future as expressed by Frank Bowling, 'I believe the black soul, if there is such a thing, belongs in Modernism' [66] (1976).

The traditional was critiqued often in the movement through satire and disdain. The latter is clear in Boyce's *Lay back, keep quiet and think of what made Britain so great* (1986), a quadriptych of three Christian crosses containing imperialised lands: South Africa, India and Australia. The fourth panel depicts Boyce herself, looking outward to the viewer with a reproving stare. As the title makes reference to 'suffering in silence', Boyce scorns Britain's ugly imperialist past, the enforced quietness of the British role in slavery, colonialism and genocide that remains untaught in our schools and is rarely acknowledged, a tactic heavily criticised by globally oppressed peoples (Goodfellow).[67] In Barbara Walker's (b.1964) striking series' *Vanishing Point* she expertly highlights black figures depicted in servitude in the margins of European historical paintings. For example, Titian's *Diana and Acteon* painting is often cited within black feminism as an example of the European undesirability attributed to black women[68] (Smith-Galer 2019).

Enlisting humour, Lubaina Himid (b.1954) creates satirical characters that challenge and mock common tropes. In *Carrot Piece* (1985) Himid refers to the belittlement of black women by white men, where a man balances on a unicycle, trying to lure the womn with a carrot on a stick. Himid's life-sized painted woodcuts presented at the *Five Black Women* 1983 exhibition, depict gratuitous male sex organs. In *Pandora's Box*, the words 'oppression' and 'war' shoot from a disturbingly oversized phallus, suggesting that the mistreatment maintained within our patriarchally ruled society is intrinsically linked to male fragility and a preoccupation with sexual dominance.

This anti-patriarchal message is also clear in Sutapa Biswas's *Housewives with Steak Knives* (1985) in which the 'servient housewife' is brought to apotheosis, referencing Hindu culture's depiction of pure feminine power, Kali Sanskrit - for 'She Who is Black/Death' Kali is depicted as sexual and violent. Biswas's 'house-wife deity' wags her tongue, in tribute to blood drinking, a string of beheaded dictators around her neck. Wielding a flag with Artemisia Gentileschi's *Judith Slaying Holofernes*, Biswas pays homage to female artists of the past. (Sherwin 2020).[69]

For women of colour, whose image is affected by colonial attitudes and racism – her battle is with visibility, as historically her depictions are fetishized and distorted (Pollock).[70] Therefore, it becomes crucial to the black women artist engaged in political-socio-economic discourse, to represent complex individuals. In creating the intention of discourse with a black feminist perspective, in attempting to empower women of colour in a disempowering world, it could be argued that *presence* above all else, is at the heart of these endeavours.

Tilda Williams-Kelly

Chapter 4

Politics, Art, and Tokenism

*"The master's tools will never
dismantle the master's house"*
Audre Lorde 1984[71]

The First National Black Art Convention at Wolverhampton University in 1979, instigated visual dialogue with UK BIPoCs[72] (Samuel 2018), influenced by the political climate of the time. This followed on from Enoch Powell's 'Rivers of Blood' speech (1968) and the subsequent 1970 Tory victory. The demonisation of immigrants by politicians and media promoted divisive tensions between the British public. The next decade in Britain was marked by periods of civil unrest. The 1981 and 1985 Brixton Race Riots were both in response to the police's treatment of black people, especially the shooting and paralysis of Cherry Groce by police in her own home[73] (Jones 2020). Birmingham artist Barbara Walker's 2006 series *Louder Than Words*, manipulates real police dockets from her son's own 'stop and search' experiences. London artist, Kimathi Donkor (b.1965) depicted Groce's shooting in his painting *Under Fire: The Shooting of Cherry Groce 2005* [74] (Philip 2015). The recession increased job uncertainty, heightening xenophobia, and rhetoric such as 'drain the swamp' became mainstream as Thatcherism spread.

In response, artists collaborated together as 'Black' creating a safe space for expression. Most were ancestrally linked to South Asia, the Caribbean and Africa. While 'Black' could be a stance of 'cultural pride' for African diaspora artists, the same cannot be true for South Asian artists resulting in misuse of the term[75] (Modood 1994). Many Asian artists including Anish Kapoor[76] chose not to use the descriptor (Balaram 2016). Founding member Keith Piper mused on their evolvement from the decade without establishing the 'deeply contested term,' legitimacy of which evokes 'a widespread weariness,' and uncertainty on its '[necessity] or [usefulness]'[77] (Piper 2002).

It is necessary for the oppressed to openly define conditions, in order to secure change. The Black Arts Movement attempted this feat and are recognised to a degree, within British postmodern history. The true failure lies in not securing real and sustained change. As Himid stated, 'We created something, named it, and then allowed it to be un-named and thus de-funded. It certainly does not exist now' [78] (Himid 2005).

Forty years later, race relations have not improved much. Following the *Black Lives Matter* protests in the US, the UK saw protests in over 150 locations, in solidarity with those murdered by the police. Global police conduct came under scrutiny, in Scotland, with the death of Sheku Bayou who was killed in Kirkcaldy police custody. This is now being re-investigated and Section 60 stop and search powers have been proven to be discriminatory and are widely condemned[79] (Keenan 2020). Other forms of previously accepted racism have been examined, including calls for the removal of glorified figures that enforced colonial rule, the statue of slave trader Edward Colvin being pulled down and thrown in Bristol Harbour by protestors[80] (2020). This highly visible, energetic and global engagement in anti-racism was unparalleled in scale, and naturally it encouraged racist backlash (Cordova 2020). Nationalists engaged in violence against peaceful protestors and police[81] (2020). These highly publicised incidents invigorated what was often viewed as an old and tired discussion. It introduced swathes of people to the messaging of antiracism activism for the first time, after its vandalism; Machache received 'overwhelming' support from the community in Dundee raising hundreds of pounds to re-install her mural[82] (Meiklem 2020). Anti-racism book sales skyrocketed in 2020, and *Why I'm No Longer Talking to White People About Race* by Reni Eddo-Lodge became a best-seller in Britain, three years after it was published[83] (Flood 2020). Inclusion of transgender people within the *BLM* movement gained traction, and Milan Nicole Sherry's slogan *Black Lives Can't Matter Until Trans Black Lives Matter* entered the mainstream movement[84] (BBC *Three* 2020). This is a topic which demands significant further attention, research and action but is not examined here. The difference between this moment and that of the 1980s lies in the power of social media and its ability to amplify voices and create global movements without the approval or consent of mainstream media.

In the same way, social media has allowed more accessible and culturally diverse art (Ali 2020), however institutionally, there is still a significant disparity in POCs within art sectors[85] (Ali 2020). As 'whiteness characterises higher education institutions', minority students report dissatisfaction within universities[86] (Joseph-Salisbury 2018) and are more likely to drop out than white students with equivalent grades from school[87] (Ardis 2020). Easily framed as 'isolated incidents', several high-ranking UK universities are publicly criticised by students for allowing misogynist and racist behaviour. Top Scottish universities are investigating this, after a black female student shared images of a group chat describing her as a 'n*****' on social media[88]

(Mitchell 2020). This kind of environment harms productive output, grades and mental health.

Diversity action, such as the *Get Up Stand Up Now* exhibit in London, shows there is more willingness to include Black artists[89] (Bakare 2019). Tate Britain has presented the work of Lynette Yiadom-Boakye in her *Fly in League with the Night* exhibit, 'the first major survey of one of the most important painters working today', which is currently on display[90] (2020-21), and Chila Kumari Singh Burman's winter commission lit up the building in lights in her installation *remembering a brave new world*, shown until late February[91] (2020-21). These showcases recognise and celebrate WOC artists. Whether this willingness to elevate their work is indicative of long-term structural change, remains to be seen. When speaking on Claudette Johnson's exhibition at Modern Art Oxford (2019), *I Came to Dance*[92] Eddie Chambers was doubtful and noted 'one of the principal problems' with the exhibition and 'the way in which Modern Art Oxford described it was that, conspicuous by its absence, was any reference as to why Johnson's work had been subject to a nearly three decades long hiatus' [93] (Chambers 2020).

In *Women Can't Paint*, Helen Gørrill reports being 'rejected by each and every institution almost immediately,' when applying for funding for intersectional research and '[found] that [she is] not alone in receiving systematic rejection of such a crucial topic' Gørrill 2020).[94] Audre Lorde's assessment on enlisting the master's tools to dismantle the house is as apt as it was in 1984, as Gørrill states,

> Museums are unlikely to fund projects that expose flaws in the system, universities are unlikely to fund projects that poke sticks at valuable external contacts and institutions are too keen to tow the line (2020, p.170) .

Art institutes have increased diversity action but fail to construct beneficial change for minority communities. With these disparities in mind we can see the challenges that face minority students and artists, and can be, in part, attributed to their lack of success within the mainstream art market.

Tilda Williams-Kelly

Conclusion

In researching the reasoning of black feminist rhetoric and relating it to the women involved in the *British Black Arts Movement*, within our current political climate of identity politics, backlash and continuous sexism in the arts: I would conclude that despite decades of discussion, the fight for presence in the rooms where decisions are made is still an unresolved issue. This will remain so until students, educators, gallerists, critics, press, museums and collectors refuse to pander to systemised disenfranchisement of marginalised groups, in aid of the egalitarian and multifaceted future of British contemporary arts.

Historically, although unnamed, misogynoir was purposefully put in place by patriarchal structures to keep black women in the role of 'damned,' and place white women in the role of 'pure,' each of these categorisations are dangerous. In modern society, people continue to perpetuate these categories largely unaware of the source of their bias and with this ignorance, they dismiss it. Minimally, this results in a lack of opportunity, life satisfaction and equal treatment. Maximally the results are abuse, exploitation and death. Intersectionality and the term misogynoir can help us rectify this and put a stop to it, if only those with educational access take interest and teach younger generations better.

The *British Black Arts Movement* ultimately failed; naivete, non-unity and a failure to document are indeed factors. However, the fault is not with a lack of talent, drive or intellect but within our institutions and education systems. Without support from funding and research bodies, engagement from critics, galleries and museums, and improved arts education, the movement could never have established itself within the British contemporary mainstream.

These artists exemplified the grit, dedication and anti-establishment commitment that the supposed liberal arts cherish. I would conclude that, although deserved, Himid's Turner win in 2017 and similarly, achievements such as Boyce representing Britain in the 2022 *Venice Biennale* are token gestures, not in that they have no meaning, to be clear, these accomplishments demonstrate serious progress. However, in doing so, these white male-led institutions have effectively allowed these 'outspoken' artists entry to the boys' club, and swiftly shut the doors behind them, silencing critics of the established regime and washing hands of actually enforcing institutional change: *What do you mean black women artists are downtrodden? Lubaina Himid just won a Turner!*

Individually, these artists have achieved a great deal, and I applaud them as they have been my role models. Yet forty, fifty, sixty years from now, will black Scottish painting students still be looking to the 1980s English Midlands for role models? Without a willingness from our institutions to combat the erasure of contributions to art history from nonwhite non-male people, then BIPoC students will continue to seek support from elsewhere. What is necessary for change is diversity within senior curatorial positions, not just community programmes, or lower-field education. Responses from institutions via token assignment are not good enough. Furthermore, as we live in an interconnected world, outward exploits should be encouraged.

My contribution to this topic is insight to a situation that can be, and is easily dismissed. As discussed in the introduction and shown within appendices, there is a growing unsafe environment on our own campus and within the UK for people of colour and those speaking out against discrimination. Students feeling entitled enough to *spit* at a staff member on campus on the basis of race, is a serious problem.

Initiatives such as the newly implemented Equality Diversity and Inclusion (EDI) focus group within Dundee University can help us first understand the mindset of those on campus, and then address serious issues. As discussed it seems ignorance is the main cause of the anger felt among a minority of white students and staff in that they misunderstand the aims and view discussions as an attack on them. The only way to combat ignorance is with knowledge, and what better place to do so than in Higher education? There is a huge gap in knowledge surrounding feminist, cultural and intersectional study that must be discussed, I hope this book has provided even just a small contribution to what I believe is a most crucial topic.

Tilda Williams-Kelly

Appendix 1

Race Charter Findings

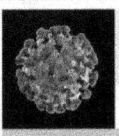

"**I have been spat at in the street.** I have been called "Corona" <u>on campus</u>" (Staff, Asian)

"A coughing sound and covering of nose and mouth can be heard and seen when I walk pass those perpetrator. This was outside of the institution. On the street, someone called me **diseased** lol". (Student, Asian)

Incident #1: 1 March 2020

"There were three of us students (Asian descent: 2 Chinese and 1 Indian) wearing masks and crossing the road towards Dundee train station. A car stopped at the traffic light and an individual coughed and spat at us, shouting at us to go back home".

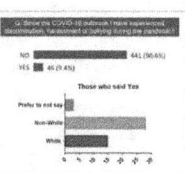

Coronavirus

Tilda Williams-Kelly

Appendix 2

University Race Charter Findings

There is greater awareness of #BLM in both students and staff communities, although comments suggest there is growing resentment and misunderstanding amongst our communities

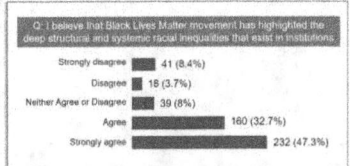 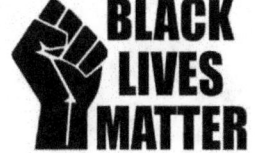

- "I'm sorry but there is far too much BLM just now. I'm fed up of being made to feel bad just because I am White".

BLM is nothing but an anti-Scottish anti-White movement and should not be tolerated on Campus. Anyone openly expressing support for it should be disciplined."

Comments by White UoD students, 2020

Tilda Williams-Kelly

Appendix 3

University Race Charter Findings

The survey comments suggests there is a growing anger and resentment against equality (from a minority of students) that needs to be addressed

"This really does boil my blood. I could not care less about being exposed to different cultures and perspectives on my course." (Student, White)

"I regard all this activity as of limited value". (Staff, ethnicity withheld).

The survey comments suggest there is an element of white supremacy culture amongst a minority of the student population…

Tilda Williams-Kelly

Appendix 4:

University Race Charter Findings

"This is ▮▮▮▮. This is our Scotland. Everything should be taught from **OUR** perspective. If **Africans and Asians don't like it they can go somewhere else.** There be absolutely **NO** pandering to BAME/POCs."

"There are no deep structural and systemic racial inequalities that exist in the ▮▮▮▮▮▮▮. If non-Whites don't like it they should leave the country."

The University ▮▮▮ must make Scottish students its prime focus and priority. And **all Scots are White**."

Tilda Williams-Kelly

Appendix 5

Vandalised Black Lives Matter Mural (Sekai Machache)

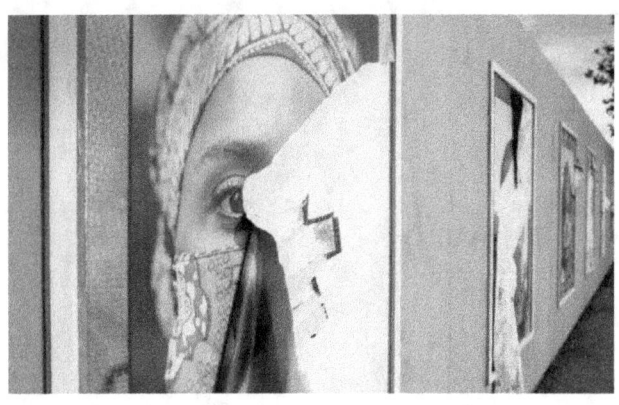

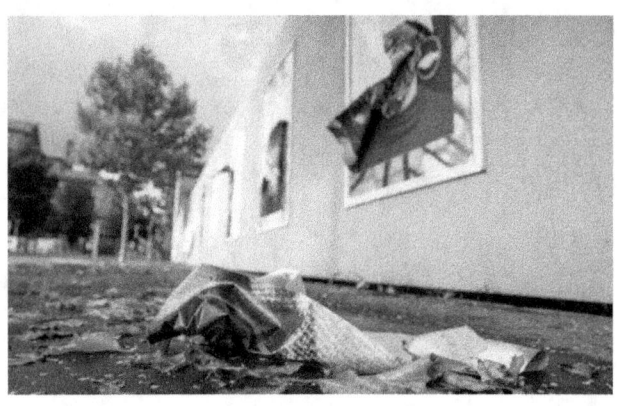

Tilda Williams-Kelly

Appendix 6
SYKE's Defaced George Floyd Mural, Hilltown, Dundee 2020

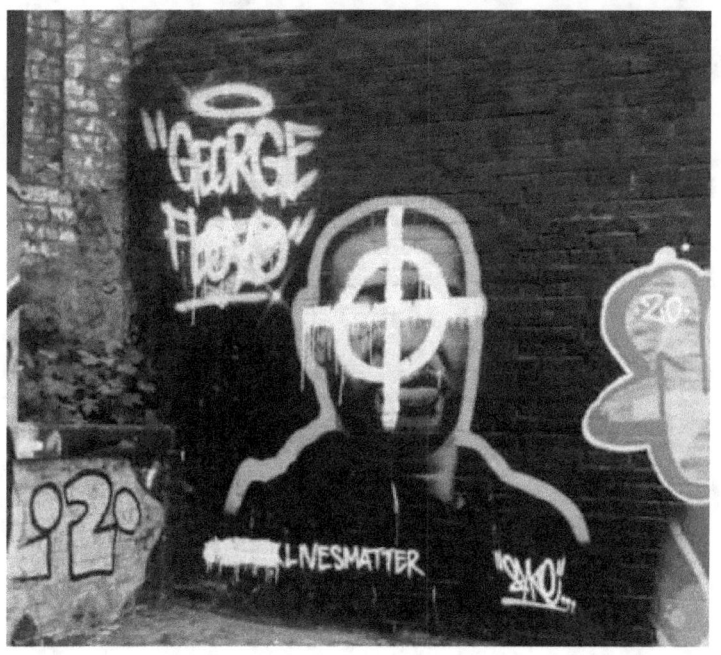

Tilda Williams-Kelly

Appendix 7

List of Artists in Lubaina Himid Curated Exhibitions

Five Black Women Artists (1983), Africa Centre, London: Sonia Boyce, Lubaina Himid, Claudette Johnson, Houria Niata and Veronica Ryan.

Black Woman Time Now (1983-4), Battersea Arts Centre, London: Brenda Agard, Sonia Boyce, Chila Kumari Burman, Jean Campbell, Margaret Cooper, Elizabeth Eugene, Lubaina Himid, Claudette Johnson, Veronica Ryan, Mumtaz Karimjee, Cherry Lawrence, Houria Niati, Ingirid Pollard, Andrea Telman and Leslie Wills.

The Thin Black Line (1985), Institute for Contemporary Arts in London: Marlene Smith, Veronica Ryan, Sonia Boyce, Claudette Johnson, Maud Sulter, Chila Burman, Brenda Agard, Sutapa Biswas, Jenifer Courie, Lubaina Himid and Ingrid Pollard.

Tilda Williams-Kelly

Appendix 8

Internet Abuse of Diane Abbott

WARNING EXPLICIT

AND ABUSIVE CONTENT

Mike Wingert @MikeWin · 4d
@HackneyAbbott @IpsosMORI
@bbcnickrobinson Why are all
Labour supporters **dirty**? Why
is **Diane abbott** so fat? She
smells badly of body
odour.....but then, her sort
always do......

Welshy @Welsh_Goo.. · 16 Apr
If ever got to jackpot question
on 5 gold rings should be **Diane
Abbott** naked and you have to
find her **cunt** #impossibleround

Lukehoostawkin... · 05 Jan 12
Diane Abbott can suck my
white cock ...racism works both
ways you fat **whore**

McShitrick @Rich... · 23 Apr
Been wondering about that
super massive **black** hole at the
centre of the galaxy. Has **Diane
Abbott** been seen recently?

M @DontCallMeMiki · 6d
Diane Abbott: Britain is racist.
Britain: no it's not you monkey
faced black **slut**!!1!1!!

The Dice Man @alex... · 02 May
Diane Abbott is comedy gold,
the useless fat **cunt**

Alex @MrBrexit_ · 6h
Is **Diane Abbott** a genuine
retard?

Markus Mohr @... · 08 Mar 12
Diane Abbott - what a **whore**

Fears Order 66 @Ya... · 02 May
All you hear bout nowadays is
"white privilege" but if you ever
want to see "**black** privilege" in
action,just know that **Diane
Abbott** is an MP

M♡♡M♡♡ · 07 May
My roast pork today was vile!!
Had more **fat** on it than **Diane
Abbott** 😂

Billy Meredith @U... · 06 May
Diane Abbott does
Countdown.

Image [95] Jack (2017) *We need to talk about Diane Abbott. Now. (EXPLICIT CONTENT)*

Appendix 9

Internet Abuse of Diane Abbott, Sexism and Racism. Examples of Abusive Tweets mentioning @HackneyAbbott

WARNING EXPLICIT

AND ABUSIVE CONTENT

> Replying to @HackneyAbbott
> this **fat** retarded black **bitch** thinks you should be forced to feed and house a bunch of violence foreign invaders. i strongly disagree.

> @HackneyAbbott Piss off you disgusting useless **fat bitch**! You're a parasite alien looking to silence native people for your power.

> Replying to @HackneyAbbott
> You forgot "fat disgusting obese chicken-loving **nigger**"

> Replying to @HackneyAbbott
> An acid attack would probably make your face look better you fat **nigger**

Insights, A. G. (2017) *Unsocial Media: Tracking Twitter Abuse against Women MPs*,

.

Appendix 10:

Diane Abbott, Abusive Tweets 1 January — 8 June / Abusive Tweets 6 weeks prior to 8 June Election 2017

		No. of Abusive Tweets	Percentage of All Abusive Tweets	MP	Political Party
Whole Period					
	1	8121	31,61%	**Diane Abbott**	Labour
	2	1025	3,9%	Joanna Cherry	SNP
	3	1023	3,9%	Emily Thornberry	Labour
	4	1002	3,9%	Jess Phillips	Labour
	5	875	3,4%	Anna Soubry	Conservative
6 Weeks Before					
	1	4512	45,14%	**Diane Abbott**	Labour
	2	458	4,58%	Emily Thornberry	Labour
	3	368	3,68%	Joanna Cherry	SNP
	4	347	3,47%	Amber Rudd	Conservative
	5	303	3,03%	Angela Rayner	Labour

Insights, A. G. (2017) *Unsocial Media: Tracking Twitter Abuse against Women MPs*,

Tilda Williams-Kelly

Bibliography

__Foreword__

1. Alice Correia, "Researching Exhibitions of South Asian Women Artists in Britain in the 1980s", British Art Studies, Issue 13, https://doi.org/10.17658/issn.2058-5462/issue-13/acorreia

Introduction

2. Bailey, M. and Trudy (2018) 'On misogynoir: citation, erasure, and plagiarism', *Feminist Media Studies*, 18(4), pp. 762–768. doi: 10.1080/14680777.2018.1447395.
3. Palmer, L. A. (2020) 'Diane Abbott, misogynoir and the politics of Black British feminism's anticolonial imperatives: "In Britain too, it's as if we don't exist"', *The Sociological Review*, 68(3), pp. 508–523. doi: 10.1177/0038026119892404.
4. *Kimberlé Crenshaw on Intersectionality, More than Two Decades Later* (2017). Available at: https://www.law.columbia.edu/news/archive/kimberle-crenshaw-intersectionality-moretwo-decades-later (Accessed: 31 January 2021).
5. Blackwell-Pal, J. (2020) 'The Black Lives Matter movement in 2020: results and prospects', *rs21*, 1 July.

Available at:
https://www.rs21.org.uk/2020/07/01/the-black-livesmatter-movement-in-2020-results-and-prospects/ (Accessed: 31 January 2021).
6. Addo, I. Y. (2020) 'Double pandemic: racial discrimination amid coronavirus disease 2019', *Social Sciences & Humanities Open*, 2(1), p. 100074. doi: 10.1016/j.ssaho.2020.100074.
7. Faludi, S. (1991). *Backlash: the undeclared war against American women.* New York, Crown
8. Adams, A. and Dalrymple, T., 2019. *Culture War: Art, Identity Politics and Cultural Entryism.*
9. *Dundee University Race Charter Focus Group* (2021). Proceedings of the student focus group 26 January 2021.
10. *Ibid.*
11. *Ibid.*
12. Mhura, W. (2020) 'BLM Mural Trail – Wezi Mhura'. Available at: https://www.wezi.uk/blm-mural-trail/ (Accessed: 14 January 2021).
13. *Ibid.*
14. Meiklem, P. J. (no date) 'Artist unveils Dundee coronavirus portraits as part of Black Lives Matter trail', *The Courier.* Available at: https://www.thecourier.co.uk/fp/news/local/dundee/1589326/ive-been-spat-at-walkingdown-the-street-artist-behind-dundee-coronavirus-portraits-opens-up-on-city-racism/ (Accessed: 7 January 2021).
15. Public Health England (August 2020) 'Disparities in the risk and outcomes of COVID-19', p. 39.

[16] Machache, S. Conversations within *YonAfro Collective* (October 2020)

[17] Rae, S. and Bell, M. (June 2020) 'Dundee mural to George Floyd defaced with "white supremacist symbol" painted over his face', *Evening Telegraph*. Available at: https://www.eveningtelegraph.co.uk/fp/dundee-muralto-george-floyd-defaced-with-shooting-target-painted-over-his-face/ (Accessed: 14 January 2021).

[18] Williamson, S. (June 10, 2020) 'Councillors across Dundee condemn George Floyd mural vandalism', *Evening Telegraph*. Available at: https://www.eveningtelegraph.co.uk/fp/councillors-across-dundee-condemngeorge-floyd-mural-vandalism/ (Accessed: 7 January 2021).

[19] Gørrill, H. (2020) *Women Can't Paint: Gender, The Glass Ceiling and Values in Contemporary Art* (p.13)

Chapter One, Literature Review

[20] Chambers, E. (2014) *Black Artists in British Art: A History since the 1950s*. Bloomsbury Publishing.

[21] Hall, S. (2006) 'Black Diaspora Artists in Britain: Three "Moments" in Post-war History', *History Workshop*. An earlier version of this argument is found in Hall's essay, 'Assembling the 80s – The Deluge and After', in Shades of Black, ed. David A. Bailey, Ian Baucom and Sonia Boyce, Durham NC, 2005.

[22] Hall, S. (2006) 'Black Diaspora Artists in Britain: Three "Moments" in Post-war History', *History Workshop Journal*, 61(1), pp. 1–24. doi: 10.1093/hwj/dbi074.

23. *Errol Lloyd, "An Historical Perpective, introduction to Caribbean Expressions in Britain, exhibition catalogue, Leicestershire Museum and Art Gallery, 16 Aug – 28 Sep 1986 pp.5-6*
24. Chambers, E. (2014) *Black Artists in British Art: A History since the 1950s.* Bloomsbury Publishing. P.128
25. *Lubaina Himid, Inside the Invisible: For/Getting Strategy, Shades of Black: Assembling Black Arts in 1980s Britain p.41*
26. Chambers, E. (2014) *Black Artists in British Art: A History since the 1950s.* Bloomsbury Publishing. P.138
27. *Lubaina Himid, Inside the Invisible: For/Getting Strategy, Shades of Black: Assembling Black Arts in 1980s Britain p.41*
28. Mercer, K. (1992) *ENGENDERED SPECIES: DANNY TISDALE AND KEITH PIPER.* Available at: https://www.artforum.com/print/199206/engendered-species-danny-tisdale-andkeith-piper-33552 (Accessed: 14 January 2021).
29. Keith Piper, *Step into the Arena: Notes on Black Masculinity & the Contest of Territory*, exhibition catalogue, Rochdale: Rochdale Art Gallery, 1991, p. 7.
30. *Lubaina Himid, Inside the Invisible: For/Getting Strategy, Shades of Black: Assembling Black Arts in 1980s Britain p.41,43*
31. Himid, L., 1990. Mapping: a decade of Black women artists 1980–1990. *Passion: Discourses on Blackwomen's Creativity*, pp.63-72.

32. Himid, "Letters to Susan," in Thin Black Line(s) (exhibition catalogue) (London: Tate Britain, 2012), 11.
33. Sulter, M. (2018) 'About Maud Sulter', *MAUD SULTER PASSION*, 24 May. Available at: https://maudsulterpassion.wordpress.com/projects/ (Accessed: 14 January 2021).
34. Bernier, Celeste-Marie (2018) *Stick to the skin: African American and Black British art, 1965-2015*. P.87

Chapter Two: Misogynoir and Intersectionality

35. Hooks, B., 1981. *Ain't I a Woman*. London: Pluto Press. P.160
36. Palmer, L. A. (2020) 'Diane Abbott, misogynoir and the politics of Black British feminism's anticolonial imperatives: "In Britain too, it's as if we don't exist"', *The Sociological Review*, 68(3), pp. 508–523. doi: 10.1177/0038026119892404.
37. Insights, A. G. (2017) *Unsocial Media: Tracking Twitter Abuse against Women MPs*, *Medium*. Available at: https://medium.com/@AmnestyInsights/unsocial-media-tracking-twitter-abuse-against-women-mpsfc28aeca498a (Accessed: 5 January 2021).
38. Berger, J. (2008). *Ways of seeing*. London, England: Penguin Classics. For importance in image see chapter 1, p.7
39. hooks, bell. (1981). *Ain't I a woman: Black women and feminism*. Boston, MA, South End Press. P. 160, 33
40. *The Mythification of the Mammy* (2018). Available at: https://web.archive.org/web/20181013102324/http:/

/xroads.virginia.edu/~MA99/diller/mammy/fiction.html (Accessed: 16 January 2021).
41. Pilgrim, D. (2008) *The Sapphire Caricature - Anti-black Imagery - Jim Crow Museum - Ferris State University.* Available at: https://www.ferris.edu/HTMLS/news/jimcrow/antiblack/sapphire.htm (Accessed: 16 January 2021).
42. Leath, S. (2019) *How the Expectation of Strength Harms Black Girls and Women, Scholars Strategy Network.* Available at: https://scholars.org/contribution/how-expectation-strength-harms-black-girls-and (Accessed: 2 January 2021).
43. *Mental health statistics: people seeking help* (2018) *Mental Health Foundation.* Available at: https://www.mentalhealth.org.uk/statistics/mental-health-statistics-people-seeking-help (Accessed: 2 January2021).
44. Cooper, J. *et al.* (2010) 'Ethnic differences in self-harm, rates, characteristics and service provision: three-city cohort study', *The British Journal of Psychiatry*, 197(3), pp. 212–218. doi: 10.1192/bjp.bp.109.072637.
45. MBRRACE-UK Maternal Report 2018 - Web Version.pdf
46. Germany, D. S., Hamburg (no date) *DER SPIEGEL | Online-Nachrichten.* Available at: https://www.spiegel.de/ (Accessed: 14 December 2020). https://www.spiegel.de/international/germany/spiegel-interview-with-german-painter-georg-baselitz-a-879397.html

47. Halperin, J. and Burns, C. (2019) *Female Artists Represent Just 2 Percent of the Market. Here's Why—and How That Can Change*, artnet News. Available at: https://news.artnet.com/womens-place-in-the-artworld/female-artists-represent-just-2-percent-market-heres-can-change-1654954 (Accessed: 2 February 2021).
48. Gørrill, H. 2020. *Women Can't Paint: Gender, The Glass Ceiling and Values in Contemporary Art.* International Library of Modern and Contemporary Art, I.B. Tauris.
49. *Sulter, Maud. Passion Discourses on Blackwomen's Creativity . Urban Fox, 1990. Print.* Preface, p.10
50. Gørril, H. 2020. *Women Can't Paint: Gender, The Glass Ceiling and Values in Contemporary Art.* International Library of Modern and Contemporary Art, I.B. Tauris. (p.16)
51. Emelife, A. (2020) *How the art world can step up for Black Lives Matter*, The Independent. Available at: https://www.independent.co.uk/arts-entertainment/art/features/black-lives-matter-art-galleries-george-floyda9561951.html (Accessed: 7 January 2021).
52. Hardi, C. (2020) 'Blaming the feminists: attempts to debilitate a movement', *LSE Women, Peace and Security blog*, 3 June. Available at: https://blogs.lse.ac.uk/wps/2020/06/03/blaming-the-feminists-attempts-to-debilitatea-movement/ (Accessed: 8 February 2021).

53. John Stuart Mill, *The Subjection of Women* (1869) in *Three Essays* by John Stuart Miff, World's Classics Series, London, 1966, p. 441.
54. Lorde, A., 2018. The Master's Tools Will Never Dismantle the Master's House. Penguin UK. (p.29)

Chapter Three: Aesthetics and Communication

55. In Barbara Thompson, Black Womanhood: Images, Icons, and Ideologies of the African Body, Seattle: University of Washington Press, 2008, 316
56. Himid, "Letters to Susan," in Thin Black Line(s) (exhibition catalogue) (London: Tate Britain, 2012), 11.
57. Basquiat, J.-M. (2010) *The artist*. Available at: http://www.basquiat.com/artist.htm (Accessed: 3 February 2021).
57. Tate (2018) *'No Woman, No Cry', Chris Ofili, 1998*, Tate. Available at: https://www.tate.org.uk/art/artworks/ofili-no-woman-no-cry-t07502 (Accessed: 3 February 2021).
58. Smith, Z. (June 2017) *Lynette Yiadom-Boakye's Imaginary Portraits*, *The New Yorker*. Available at: https://www.newyorker.com/magazine/2017/06/19/lynette-yiadom-boakyes-imaginary-portraits (Accessed: 11 January 2021).
59. Jennifer Higgie, "A Life in a Day," 91. Also: Bernier, Celeste-Marie, 2018. *Stick to the skin: African American and Black British art*, 1965-2015. (p.240)

60. Frederica, Brooks. *Ancestral Links: The Art of Claudette Johnson* in *Passion: Discourses on Blackwomen's Creativity* p.183
61. Claudette Johnson, quoted in Himid, *Claudette Johnson*, p. 2
62. Lizzie Carey-Thomas and Paul Goodwin, "Interview with Sonia Boyce and Christine Woods," in *Migrations: Journeys in British Art*, ed. Lizzie Carey-Thomas (London: Tate, 2012), 114.
63. Sara Selwood, Sonia Boyce, and Pitika Ntuli, *Sonia Boyce: Air*, n.p.
64. Lizzie Carey-Thomas and Paul Goodwin, "Interview with Sonia Boyce," in *Migrations: Journeys in British Art,* ed. Lizzy Carey-Thomas (London: Tate, 2012), 114.
65. Frank Bowling, *Frank Bowling and Bill Thompson: a Conversation Between Two Painters*, Art International, 1976, quoted in Rasheed Araeen, The Other Story, London, 1989.
66. Goodfellow, M. (2019) *Put Britain's colonial history on the curriculum – then we'll know who we really are | Maya Goodfellow, the Guardian.* Available at: http://www.theguardian.com/commentisfree/2019/dec/05/britain-colonial-history-curriculum-racism-migration (Accessed: 22 December 2021).
67. Galer, S. S. (2019) *How black women were whitewashed by art.* Available at: https://www.bbc.com/culture/article/20190114-how-black-women-were-whitewashed-by-art (Accessed: 3 December 2021).

[68.] Sherwin, S., 2020. Sutapa Biswas's Housewives With Steak-Knives: avenging goddess [WWW Document]. the Guardian. URL http://www.theguardian.com/artanddesign/2020/aug/21/sutapa-biswas-housewives-withsteak-knives (accessed 1.24.21).

Chapter Four: Politics, Art and Tokenism

[69.] Pollock, G. (1992) *Painting, feminism, history*. na.
[70.] Lorde, A., 2018. The Master's Tools Will Never Dismantle the Master's House. Penguin UK. (p.29)
[71.] Samuel, C. (2018) *The BLK Art Group*, *Black History Month 2021*. Available at: https://www.blackhistorymonth.org.uk/article/section/real-stories/the-blk-art-group/ (Accessed: 10 February 2021).
[72.] Jones, S., 2020. Cherry Groce: Mum's police shooting "robbed me of my childhood." BBC News.
[73.] February 18 2015, K., Philip, 2015. An Interview with Kimathi Donkor [WWW Document]. Lacuna Magazine. URL https://lacuna.org.uk/openlacuna/2541/ (accessed 9.22.20).
[74.] Modood, T. (1994) *Political Blackness and British Asians - Tariq Modood, 1994*. Available at: https://journals.sagepub.com/doi/abs/10.1177/0038038594028004004 (Accessed: 30 December 2020).

75. Balaram, R. (2016) 'With the Void, Full Powers: Anish Kapoor and the Venice Biennale of 1990', *British Art Studies*, (3). doi: https://doi.org/10.17658/issn.2058-5462/issue-03/rbalaram.
76. January 2002, Keith Piper on 'black art' and the 80s, *Wait, Did I Miss Something? Some Personal Musings on the 1980s and Beyond.* Shades of Black: Assembling Black Arts in 1980s Britain.
77. Lubaina Himid, *Inside the Invisible: For/Getting Strategy, Shades of Black: Assembling Black Arts in 1980s Britain* p.41
78. Keenan, M. (2020) *Stop and Search: can we continue to justify the use of this police power? | Diversity Matters | Kingsley Napley.* Available at: https://www.kingsleynapley.co.uk/insights/blogs/diversitymatters/stop-and-search-can-we-continue-to-justify-the-use-of-this-police-power (Accessed: 3 February 2021).
79. Khan, R. (2020) *Opinion: Tower Hamlets' monument to slave owner Robert Milligan is past due for removal, The Independent.* Available at: https://www.independent.co.uk/voices/edward-colston-statue-bristol-slaveryrobert-milligan-tower-hamlets-a9555846.html (Accessed: 1 February 2021).
80. Campbell, L. and Gayle, D. (2020) 'UK protests: Far-right demonstrators clash with London police – as it happened', *The Guardian*, 13 June. Available at: https://www.theguardian.com/world/live/2020/jun/13/uknews-live-patel-warns-of-health-and-legal-risks-at-blm-protests-coronavirus (Accessed: 1 February 2021).

81. Meiklem, P. J. (2020) 'Hundreds donated to replace Dundee Black Lives Matter exhibit ruined by vandals', *The Courier*. Available at: https://www.thecourier.co.uk/fp/news/local/dundee/1632562/hundreds-donated-toreplace-dundee-black-lives-matter-exhibit-ruined-by-vandals/ (Accessed: 1 February 2021).
82. Flood, A. (2020) *Anti-racist book sales surge in US and Britain after George Floyd killing, the Guardian*. Available at: http://www.theguardian.com/books/2020/jun/03/anti-racist-book-sales-surge-us-uk-george-floydkilling-robin-diangelo-white-fragility (Accessed: 1 February 2021).
83. *Black Trans Lives Matter: 'We're tired of having to pick sides'* (2020) *BBC Three*. Available at: https://www.bbc.co.uk/bbcthree/article/33ab8fbd-792f-44ee-85de-5dd3894f60bf (Accessed: 2 February 2021).
84. Ali, R. (2020) *Why you don't see many black and ethnic minority faces in cultural spaces – and what happens if you call out the system*, *The Conversation*. Available at: http://theconversation.com/why-you-dont-see-manyblack-and-ethnic-minority-faces-in-cultural-spaces-and-what-happens-if-you-call-out-the-system-128792
(Accessed: 2 February 2021).
85. Joseph-Salisbury, R. (2018) *Whiteness characterises higher education institutions – so why are we surprised by racism?*, *The Conversation*. Available at: http://theconversation.com/whiteness-characterises-

86. highereducation-institutions-so-why-are-we-surprised-by-racism-93147 (Accessed: 9 January 2021).
86. Ardis, M. (2020) *Drop-Out Rates Higher for Minority Students – The Gryphon*. Available at: https://www.thegryphon.co.uk/2020/02/17/drop-out-rates-higher-for-minoritystudents/?fbclid=IwAR1MvvPcc29tlcHNtXfC0MH-qgQsKej4iBB48CBsBAay9-JoOmdgf1VD0aY (Accessed: 9 January 2021).
87. Mitchell, H. (2020) *Top Scots universities investigating students for vile racist chat comments, edinburghlive*. Available at: https://www.edinburghlive.co.uk/news/edinburgh-news/top-scots-universities-investigating-after-18534887 (Accessed: 9 January2021).
88. *UK galleries have embraced black artists, says exhibition curator* (2019) *the Guardian*. Available at: http://www.theguardian.com/artanddesign/2019/jun/11/uk-galleries-have-embraced-black-artists-saysexhibition-curator-zak-ove (Accessed: 3 January 2021).
89. Tate (2020-2021) *Lynette Yiadom-Boakye: Fly In League With The Night – Exhibition at Tate Britain, Tate*. Available at: https://www.tate.org.uk/whats-on/tate-britain/exhibition/lynette-yiadom-boakye (Accessed: 11 January 2021).
90. Tate (2020-2021) *Lynette Yiadom-Boakye: Fly In League With The Night – Exhibition at Tate Britain, Tate*. Available at: https://www.tate.org.uk/whats-on/tate-britain/exhibition/lynette-yiadom-boakye (Accessed: 11 January 2021).

91. *https://www.modernartoxford.org.uk/event/claudette-johnson/* (2019) *Modern Art Oxford*. Available at: https://www.modernartoxford.org.uk/event/claudette-johnson/ (Accessed: 11 February 2021).
92. *Eddie Chambers :: Reflections (2020)*. Available at: http://www.eddiechambers.com/texts/reflections/ (Accessed: 2 February 2021).
93. Gørrill, H. (2020) *Women Can't Paint: Gender, The Glass Ceiling and Values in Contemporary Art* (p.13)
94. Jack (2017) 'We need to talk about Diane Abbott. Now. (EXPLICIT CONTENT)', *Jack Monroe*, 7 June. Available at: https://cookingonabootstrap.com/2017/06/07/we-need-to-talk-about-diane-abbott-now-explicitcontent/ (Accessed: 5 February 2021).

Sister Painter

Artist's images

Tilda Williams-Kelly

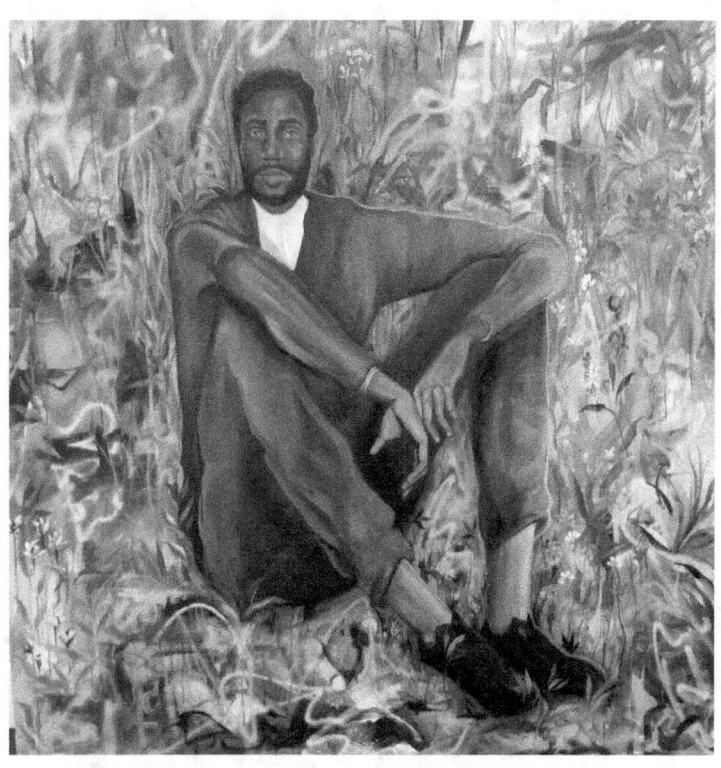

Tilda Williams-Kelly, *Portrait of Joseph Knight*, acrylic, oil and spray paint on canvas (2021) 190x190cm

Tilda Williams-Kelly

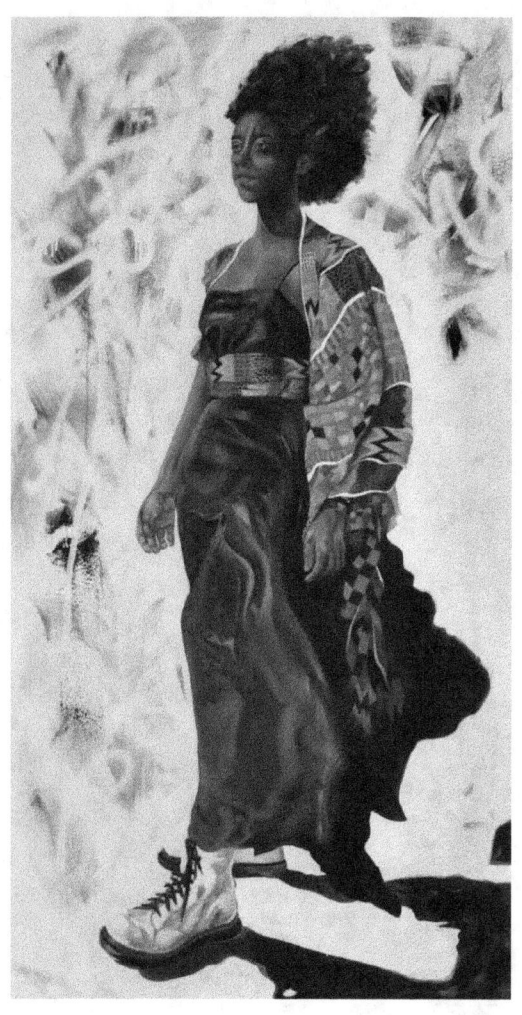

Tilda Williams-Kelly, *Against the Wind in Kente Cloth*, acrylic, oil and spray paint on canvas (2021) 150x80cm

Tilda Williams-Kelly

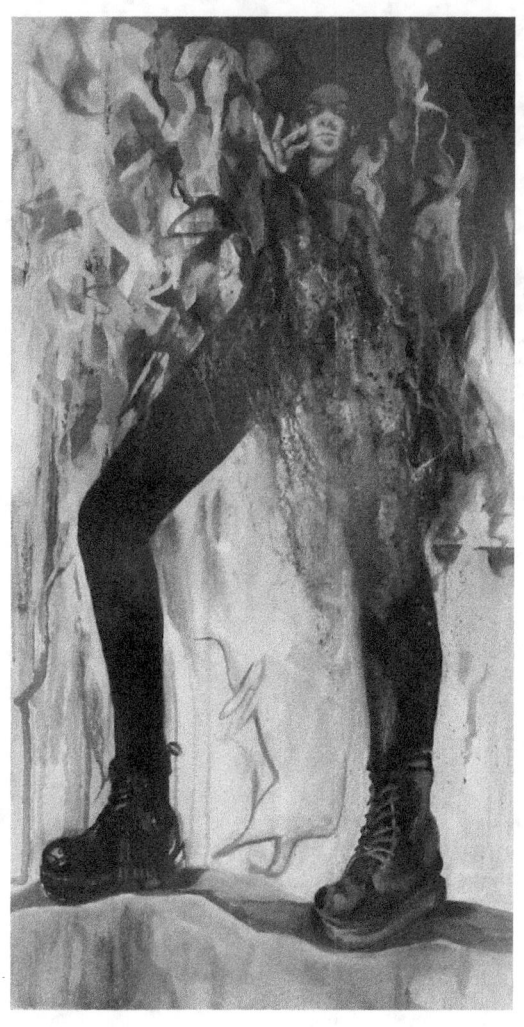

Tilda Williams-Kelly, *Shrouded Druid in Boots*, acrylic and oil on canvas (2021) 150x80cm

Tilda Williams-Kelly

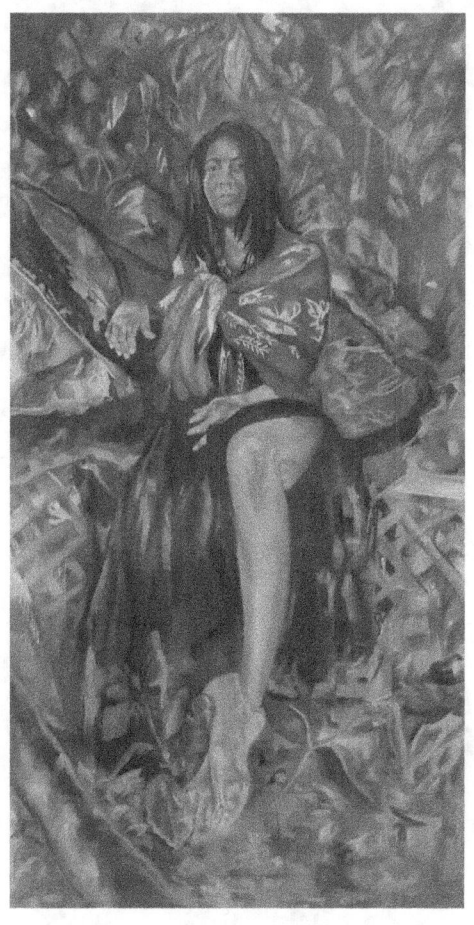

Tilda Williams-Kelly, *Light Scatters in the Cherry Laurel*, oil on canvas (2021) 150x80cm

Tilda Williams-Kelly

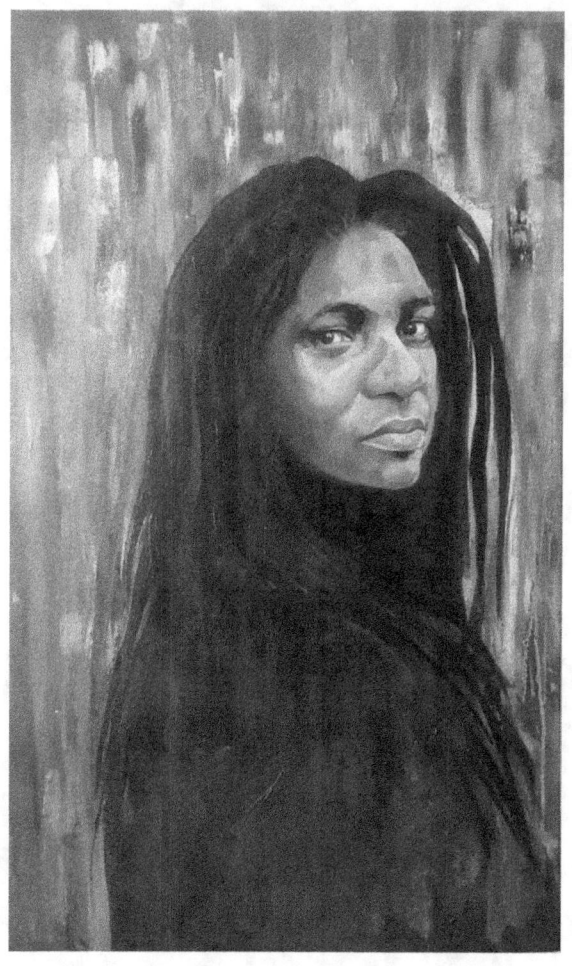

Tilda Williams-Kelly, *Sand and Brownstone*, oil on canvas (2021) 50x80cm

Tilda Williams-Kelly

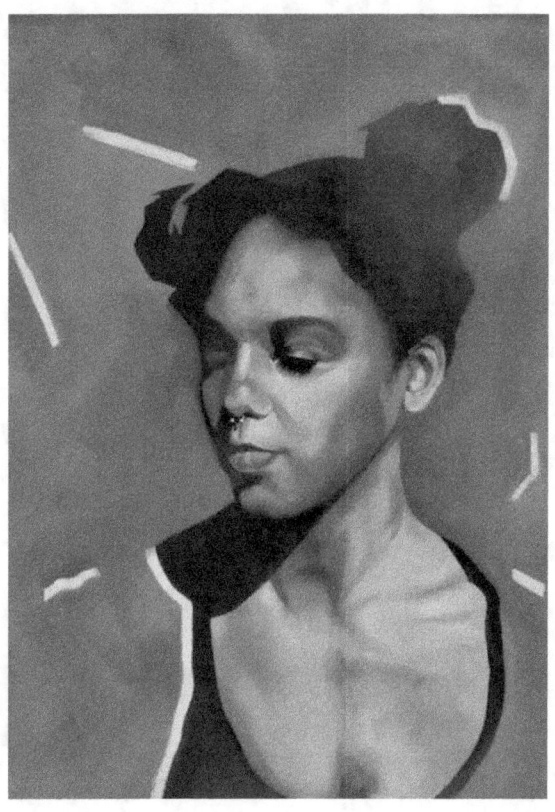

Tilda Williams-Kelly, *Blood Orange Lightstrip*, acrylic and oil on canvas (2021) 41x56cm

Tilda Williams-Kelly

Acknowledgements

I would like to thank my academic supervisor for this paper, Helen Gørrill for her continued encouragement and support of my research and refreshing contributions to feminist thinking in her inspiring book *Women Can't Paint*.

To Wezi Mhura, for giving myself and my own a platform to express our joy, and our pain as Black and Asian Scots, for putting us in contact and connecting our practices.

To Sekai Machache and Saoirse Anis who came into my life when I needed them most, for understanding the necessity in upholding, protecting, and fighting for Black women's creativity and for reminding me of it whenever I faltered.

For all the women of *YonAfro*, for immediately welcoming, understanding and valuing me.

For the friends I've made this year, for our discussions on the nature of our practices, and that which is important to us.

To my big sister for the value of never giving up, always speaking out, and fighting for stifled voices.

Finally, my mother. The first black woman artist to inspire me, whose support has left me in no doubt of my own potential as an artist, for whom I owe everything.

A note about Boom Graduates

We propel graduates forward so they can make their mark on the world - we push the boundaries, share brilliant ideas and inspire possibility. We publish dissertations as books, presented gift-boxed at graduation ceremonies, delivering brand-new research to the world quicker than anyone else. We plant trees for every commissioned book sold, and give our Boom graduates the chance to profit-share from their brilliant ideas. Furthermore we donate the majority of our profits to funding research and scholarship for disadvantaged students who wouldn't normally be able to attend university. Through academic excellence and environmental sustainability, *Boom Graduates* are changing the world.

We are Boom Graduates - an imprint of Boom Publications Ltd. We are a more-than-profit company, dedicating over half our profits to providing university scholarships for underprivileged students across the world. We aim to become the globe's biggest provider of such scholarships – and if like Tilda, the author of this book, you'd also like to contribute to making the world a better place, please contact us: we publish monographs, edited books, and moreover our graduate series – Boom Graduates – are presented at graduation days across the world in archival, lined museum-quality presentation cases, engraved with the graduate's name and award.

Boom Publications are based at the Duncan of Jordanstone College of Art and Design, at the University of Dundee in Scotland. We were one of the winners of the 2022 Venture awards hosted by the Centre for Entrepreneurship, and have since been shortlisted for the Converge Challenge, a national award that brings together ambitious and creative thinkers with innovative ideas to work with industry experts to transform their ideas into sustainable companies operating in the commercial world. We are also climate conscious and work with agencies to plant a tree for each and every book commissioned, offsetting thousands of tonnes of carbon each year. Follow us on social media to watch our forest grow @boomgraduates.

Thank you for contributing by purchasing this book. Please visit our catalogues on www.boompublications.com.

Tilda Williams-Kelly

BOOM!

This book was originally submitted as a dissertation in partial fulfilment of the requirements of a Bachelor of Arts (Hons) degree in Fine Art at the Duncan of Jordanstone College of Art and Design, the University of Dundee, in 2022.

Tilda Williams-Kelly

Notes

Tilda Williams-Kelly

Sister Painter

Tilda Williams-Kelly

Sister Painter

Tilda Williams-Kelly

Sister Painter

Tilda Williams-Kelly

Sister Painter

Tilda Williams-Kelly

Sister Painter

Tilda Williams-Kelly

www.ingramcontent.com/pod-product-compliance
Lightning Source LLC
Chambersburg PA
CBHW071416210526
45465CB00001B/408